ELEVATE

THE

Wisdom

OF Runes

Uncover the answers within

Published by Hinkler Pty Ltd
45–55 Fairchild Street,
Heatherton Victoria Australia
www.hinkler.com

hinkler

Author: Shauna Reid
Internal design: Lisa Robertson
Cover design and illustrations: Rachael Jorgensen

Images © Hinkler Pty Ltd or Shutterstock.com

ISBN: 978 1 4889 0427 1

Printed and bound in Malaysia

ELEVATE

THE
Wisdom
OF Runes

Uncover the answers within

Shauna Reid

hinkler

CONTENTS

Introduction

In this busy modern world, it's easy to get disconnected from your thoughts and feelings. With eternally chirping phones and scrolling news feeds there have never been so many opinions and options vying for your attention. This can mean that when it comes to making choices or tackling challenges, it's hard to separate the outside influences from your own true desires.

Runes are a fabulous way to cut through the noise and reconnect to your intuition. When you take a quiet moment to work with runes and interpret their timeless insights, you can strip away the overwhelming noise and hear the wise voice inside that knows just what to do.

So, what exactly are runes? They're the angular symbols that make up a runic alphabet, a system of writing that was used by ancient Germanic peoples. These days they're best known for their deeper and more magical purpose as a form of divination.

Like tarot or astrology, runes are a tool to help you uncover hidden knowledge. For centuries people have turned to them for a dose of guidance and inspiration. Each rune symbolises an aspect of life's mysteries, struggles and joys, from relationships and money to purpose and passion.

You can ask the runes questions of all kinds, from *Should I date that guy*? to *What is my life's purpose*? Your readings will help you notice patterns, make connections and explore options. Expect 'ah-ha' moments aplenty!

This book is a beginner guide to runes and all the wisdom and goodness they can bring to your life. In the following pages, you'll learn everything you need to know to get started. We'll explore:

- **The history of runes.** Discover their fascinating origins, from ancient myths and Viking inscriptions to modern divination.
- **How runes can help you today.** These ancient symbols contain deep insights and meanings that shed light on modern life.
- **Getting started with runes.** Find out what gear you'll need to begin, including how to choose your first rune set (or make your own!).
- **How to use runes.** You'll learn how to prepare your space and your mind, then explore five fabulous rune spreads to get you started on your rune journey.
- **The meanings of runes.** Demystify all those lines and squiggles so you can interpret your readings and start hearing what your intuition has to say.

The beauty of runes is that you can work with them in a way that suits you. You can ask big, deep questions to tackle complex life issues, or just pull a single rune for a quick dose of inspiration to start your day. Take this centuries-old tradition and make it your own.

Let's get started!

A history of runes

Runes have a rich and fascinating history that began more than 2000 years ago. The word 'rune' has origins in several languages - and means a variation of *secret, mystery* and *whisper*, echoing their mysterious nature. Let's look at how these timeless symbols evolved.

What are runes?

Runes are the angular symbols that make up a runic alphabet, a system of writing that was developed and used by the ancient Germanic peoples of Northern Europe. Historians still debate their precise origins, but a popular theory is that the first runic alphabet was developed by the Goths from the Etruscan alphabet of northern Italy and was likely also influenced by the Latin alphabet in the 1st or 2nd century BCE.

Runic letters are made up of vertical lines, known as staves, and branches that jut upwards, downwards, diagonally or in a curve. They were carved mainly on stone, wood, bone and metal.

Runic alphabets were multi-functional – they were both *phonetic* symbols representing spoken sounds and *visual* symbols of different elements of the natural world.

How runes were used

The runic alphabet was used more for commemorative purposes than for everyday communication. We know from the thousands of runestones discovered across northern Europe and Scandinavia that rune inscriptions were used to honour important events, people and beliefs.

While early Germanic tribes first developed runes, it was the Vikings who led their spread across Europe and beyond. Wherever the Vikings roamed, the runes came too! Inscriptions have been found as far away as England, Greenland, Russia and Turkey. The Vikings would inscribe great stone monuments that commemorated mighty leaders and their heroic achievements, as well as everyday objects like jewellery, coins and weapons. They also inscribed graves to ensure the departed had a safe passage to the afterlife.

The Elder Futhark alphabet

Across the centuries the runic alphabet evolved into different letterforms and alphabets. The most enduring alphabet and the one most frequently used in modern rune practices is the Elder Futhark. That's also the alphabet we'll explore in this book.

The Elder Futhark contains 24 symbols, which are divided into three categories of eight letters, known as an *aett*. The name 'Futhark' is derived from the first six letters of the alphabet: *Fehu, Uruz, Thurisaz, Ansuz, Raidho* and *Kaunaz*.

Like Japanese or Chinese characters, each rune is a pictorial representation of a specific object and has associated ideas and words. We'll dive into these in detail in the coming chapters.

The enduring wisdom of runes

As Christianity spread, runic alphabets were replaced by the Latin alphabet we know today. But the runic symbols themselves have lived on. Why? Because long before they functioned as written letters in an alphabet, runic symbols were used for more magical purposes.

In ancient times runes were considered to be divinely inspired symbols that held the secrets of the universe. As well as representing an object or idea, the rune also held the power of its meaning. It was believed that writing, wearing, or saying the name of a rune would activate its inherent qualities.

While there's no direct historical documentation of runes used in divination, the appearance of runes on artefacts like talismans, weapons and jewellery points to their use in spiritual practices. Runes were used for divination, for protection, for good luck, as a blessing or for cursing, as well as a means of communicating with the dead. So, whether it was an ancient farmer hoping for a fruitful harvest, or a Viking warrior inscribing his sword to protect him in battle, throughout history people have sought wisdom from runes.

The stuff of legends

Norse mythology has many tales about the divine origins of the runes, the most famous perhaps being the story of how Odin 'discovered' the runes' wisdom.

It was said that only the Norns could read and interpret the runes, mere gods and humans could not. Odin, a revered god and knowledge-seeker, was on a determined quest to find their meaning.

The poem *Hávamál* describes Odin's dramatic act of self-sacrifice. He speared himself to the Yggdrasil, the sacred ash tree, with his own sword. He hung upside down for nine days, refusing food and water until finally the secrets of the runes were revealed to him in the Well of Fate below. He then passed this wisdom to the gods and his people.

Wounded I hung on a windswept gallows
For nine long nights, pierced by a spear
Pledged to Odin, offered myself to myself
I hung upon Yggdrasil
None brought me bread
None gave me mead
Down to the depths I searched
Until I spied the Runes
I seized them up
And, screaming, I fell...

While such a tale is a world away from our modern lives, what we share with Odin is a desire for deeper wisdom and understanding of ourselves and the world around us. Whether you decide to approach your rune practice with a pragmatic and practical mindset or with a touch of magic, it's a comfort to know that people have been doing the same for thousands of years.

How runes can help you today

While we're no longer sailing the seas on longships or carving runes into giant monoliths, we share many of the basic hopes, dreams and worries about life that our ancient ancestors did. The human need for answers, or to seek advice on which path to choose, is an eternal one.

The locations and technology may have evolved, but we wrestle with similar questions, big and small. *Will I be successful? Do I need to find a new flatmate? How can I find true love? What is my place in the world?*

The runes address fundamental qualities and aspects of happiness, progress, passion, health, wealth and healing. So, when you come to them with a modern dilemma, they can offer insights that are just as relevant as they were centuries ago.

Working with runes is a way of pausing to hear your inner wisdom, without the noise of others' opinions or influence. When you reflect on what the runes present, you can find new perspectives. Sometimes a matter that's been puzzling for weeks becomes clear in an instant.

Runes are a form of modern divination

Divination is an art or practice that seeks to foretell future events or discover hidden knowledge. Other popular modern forms include tarot, crystal gazing and astrology.

There are no records of the exact ways runes were used for divination purposes in past centuries. Modern rune work tends to take the form of 'castings' or 'spreads', similar to how tarot cards are used, where runes are laid out in set positions then interpreted. It's said that when you cast the runes, they're not random but are choices that have been made by your subconscious.

Runes are guides, not fortune-tellers

Rune reading isn't used to predict the future. Instead, it's a way to access your subconscious mind and receive guidance for a particular problem, question or issue. You won't receive specific advice, but rather suggestions of potential outcomes or paths. Runes can hint towards answers while leaving you to figure out the details. They're a means of revealing the 'hidden knowledge' that's already inside you.

Runes are empowering!

Runes are a happy reminder that the future isn't fixed. You have the power to choose your path and make your own decisions. If you don't like the guidance that a rune reading provides, you can decide to change course! While runes won't change your past, they can help you understand it. And while they won't predict your future, they can help you make more informed decisions that will shape it.

Getting started with runes

It's time to gather your supplies! In this chapter, we'll look at finding your first rune set (or how to make your own!) and get ready to start using it.

Choosing your rune set

You'll need an Elder Futhark or Viking set of runes that includes all 24 runes. Some sets also include a 25th rune which is blank.

Rune sets are widely available at new age shops and online retailers. You'll find sets made of wood, stone, metal and crystals. For something special you could invest in an artisan-made set – you'll find them on independent websites or on Etsy. If you're after a modern twist, you can buy tarot-style cards or even download a smartphone app!

The important thing is that your runes feel good and right to you, so take your time when choosing.

Make your own runes

If you can't find a set of runes that sing to you, try making your own. Some say this is the ideal option, as the act of creation helps you feel more connected to the runes and your energy will be poured into them. It can also be a budget-friendly way to go!

You will need 25 pieces of your chosen material. They should be of even size and shape.

Traditionally, rune sets were made with natural materials. This is a great excuse to get outside and get foraging! Just be sure to be respectful of the environment and don't take anything that disrupts or damages the land.

Here are some material options for your DIY rune set. Let your choice be guided by what feels good and natural to you, as you'll be spending a lot of time with the finished product!

- Stones
- Pebbles
- Seashells
- Crystals or gemstones
- Wood (such as slices of a tree branch or wooden dowel)
- Paper or cardboard

Once you've got your chosen materials the next step is to carve or write the rune symbols. If you're writing them, you can use paint, a permanent marker pen or even nail polish.

Practise writing the symbols first on paper, referring to the chart in this book (see pages 44–45). Focus your mind on the task and say the name of each rune aloud as you carve or paint them, so you start getting to know them.

Consecrating your runes

Whether your runes are DIY or pre-made, you may wish to consecrate them. While this literally means 'to make holy', consecration is a small ritual that dedicates the runes to their new purpose. It elevates them above mere inanimate objects and strengthens your bond with them. This is entirely optional – some magical practitioners say it's unnecessary.

There are scores of different rituals you can do, or you could invent your own. If it feels right, try one of these...

- Bury the runes in the earth overnight.
- Leave the runes out in the sunshine for a day.
- Light sage or a candle. Place your runes to your left and focus your mind. Pick up a rune, say its name aloud, briefly meditate on its meaning, then pass it over the sage smoke or candle flame. Place it on the right side then repeat with the rest of your runes.

Storing runes

Runes are often stored in a small drawstring bag so they're kept clean and together, and so you can shake the runes before use to randomise them. You can purchase rune pouches or make your own if you're handy with a sewing machine. While red or black are traditional, choose a colour and fabric that you're drawn to. If you don't fancy keeping the runes in a bag, a small box would work well too. Again, this is all about choosing something that feels right for you.

Using a casting cloth

It's traditional to work with runes on a white rune cloth, rather than directly onto a table or other surface. The cloth acts as a boundary for the runes and, more practically, prevents them from getting damaged or dirty. You could use a dedicated cloth, but a simple napkin or tea towel is fine too.

Create a rune journal

There's a lot to learn when you start working with runes, so it's a good idea to keep a record of your journey on paper.

- **It helps you remember the details.** When you're new to runes, sometimes the wisdom of a reading won't be apparent right away. It can take days or weeks of subconscious pondering before its full significance becomes clear. By writing down the details of readings in the moment, you can refer back to them at any time.
- **You'll notice recurring themes.** As your journal pages fill over time, you may also notice patterns that help you see what's really on your mind, or what you might need to pay more attention to.
- **It's fun!** It's a pleasure to leaf back through old journal entries and see how your thoughts and interpretations have developed over time.

As with choosing your rune set, pick a journal that feels good. Whether it's a fancy leather notebook or loose-leaf paper in a folder, anything goes! It will be your trusty companion on your runic journey, so it should be something you look forward to spending time with.

Whenever you do a rune reading, make a new entry in your journal. You can include:

- The date and time of the reading.
- Your intention or the question you asked the runes.
- A quick sketch of the rune(s) drawn and their position.
- Your observations, interpretations and reflections.

Any incidental details you'd like to record: the weather, how you were feeling before the reading, any events happening in your life or the wider world at the time. It's all about you!

You may also wish to leave a little space after each entry in case you want to add more detail later once the wisdom of the reading becomes clearer, or to write about how events unfolded afterwards.

How to use runes

There are two main ways of using the runes. First, there is the traditional divination method of 'casting', where runes are thrown into a circle then interpreted. The second is rune spreads, where runes are randomly drawn then arranged into a set formation that's similar to tarot. In this book, we focus on the second method as it's great for beginners!

First, create a calm and sacred place

Before you touch a single rune it's important to create the right setting and atmosphere. This will help quieten your mind and make you feel more present, which are the keys to getting the most out of a rune reading.

- **Choose a quiet time when you're not in a hurry.** Ask your family or housemates not to disturb you. Switch off your phone.
- **Pick a calm and uncluttered spot.** Clear a flat surface for laying out your runes, like a coffee table or desk.
- **Add creature comforts.** Decorate the space with any happy-making objects like crystals or a favourite indoor plant for a connection to nature. Choose a comfy chair or cushion to sit on.
- **Create some atmosphere.** Light a candle, burn incense, or diffuse some essential oils. If it's not distracting, put on some soft background music for a calm vibe.
- **Grab your rune journal** and keep it close at hand. Don't forget your favourite pen!

It can be a good idea to work with runes in the same setting each time. Your mind will associate the two things together and it will become easier to slip into 'rune mode'! That said, runes are highly portable and it can be fun to try different settings. Reading runes outdoors for instance, whether it be in your backyard or on a quiet beach, can be wonderful for body, mind and spirit.

Get in the zone!

Once your space is prepared, get focused. Put on comfy clothing and make sure you're well-hydrated so you won't be distracted by any physical discomfort. You may like to indulge in some feel-good extras, like popping on your favourite lipstick, having a pot of herbal tea or a glass of sparkling water on hand, or draping a soft and cosy blanket over your lap. These little flourishes are a signal to yourself and the runes that you mean business!

Clear your mind

To get the most out of your reading it's important to set aside everyday thoughts first. That way you're best placed to tap into your intuition and interpret the runes before you.

To bring yourself into the moment, close your eyes and take some deep, slow breaths. Feel your body relax with each exhalation. Allow any thoughts of everyday chores or worries to pass across your mind. Imagine them dissolving into the air. Feel your feet on the floor, anchoring you to the earth.

Set an intention

It's essential to begin with an intention or question in mind so that your reading has a clear purpose.

You can do a rune reading for any reason. You might be at a crossroads in life or having trouble making a decision. You could be looking for insights to understand someone's actions or intentions, or perhaps you just want to get an inkling of what the day ahead will bring.

Whatever is on your mind, the runes can offer a listening ear and some insights on any aspect of life from career, relationships (romantic, family, friends or colleagues) and home, to health, finances and lifestyle issues. You just need to bring an open mind that's ready to explore the possibilities!

If you are looking for a general overview of a particular issue, decide on an intention. It could be, 'I want to dive into how I feel about my career path' or 'Iwant to explore my relationship with my best friend'. When you come to interpret the runes, look at how they relate to different aspects of that theme.

If you have a specific question, make sure it's a good one! Remember, runes don't predict the future. They help you look at what's happening in the present and how the past has influenced it, as well as showing you possible outcomes and options. So instead of asking a straight-up Yes or No question, keep it open-ended and expansive. This way the runes can help you explore different angles.

For example, instead of asking, 'Should I accept this job offer?' you could ask, 'What are the pros and cons of this new opportunity?'. Rather than asking, 'Was my partner totally in the wrong in our argument?' try something like, 'What do I need to know about this conflict we're having?'.

Here are some question formats to help spark useful answers:

- What do I need to consider about…?
- What are the pros and cons of…?
- What is Person X's perspective on…?
- What would help me understand my relationship with…?
- What could be the benefits of…?
- What would be the challenges of…?

Let's begin!

Take another deep breath and shake the rune bag so the runes are well mixed. Hold your question or intention in your mind as you take the first rune out of the bag and place it on the surface in front of you. If you're doing a multi-rune spread (see pages 34–38), draw the remaining runes required in the same way and place them in their designated positions.

Now look at the runes. Let your intuition lead the way – notice the images, words and feelings that pop into your mind, and any sensations you feel in your body. Read the corresponding rune descriptions in this book and think about how they relate to your intention. Remember that the meanings tend to be more metaphorical than literal. If it's a multi-rune spread, consider each rune and how their meanings connect. They may describe something you've been feeling, or help you join the dots on a matter.

Don't worry if nothing comes to you right away! Write down the position and meaning of the runes in your journal, along with any first impressions. Now put away your runes and go about your day. You may find your subconscious comes up with something later. In a quiet moment check your journal entry again to see if any new insights have surfaced.

Keep practising!

It takes time and practice to build a relationship with the runes, so be patient and kind with yourself. The best way to get more insights is to work with the runes regularly and journal the results. Over time you'll notice patterns and connections. As you get more familiar with the meanings of each rune, your own interpretations will form and you'll need to refer to this book less frequently.

Readings for others

Once you're more comfortable with the runes, you might want to start reading them for others! It's a great way to deepen your connection to your friends and family!

Follow the same process of setting the scene and clearing of everyday thoughts before you begin. Shake the rune bag to randomise the runes, then pass it to your friend. Ask them to give the bag another shake as they think of their intention or question. Now take the bag back, draw the runes and lay them out in your friend's chosen spread. Take your time looking up the rune interpretations together and chatting about what you see. Two minds can be even more insightful than one!

Using rune spreads

Here are five rune spreads to try. They range from a simple single-rune draw that's perfect for daily guidance to more complex spreads for when you're after deeper insights.

We recommend starting with the single-rune draw and working your way up through the more detailed spreads in this chapter. Once you're feeling confident with those you can even experiment with creating your own.

Whichever spread you choose, remember to always set an intention, settle yourself with a deep calming breath and keep an open mind.

Single-rune draw

Drawing a single rune is the most common way to begin a rune reading. You can use it for guidance on a quick question, to set an intention for meditation or to find a prompt for a journalling session. Another fun practice is a morning ritual of pulling a 'Rune of the Day' to gain insight into the day ahead.

You can also draw a single rune as a temperature check of sorts before diving into a multi-rune spread. Once you have interpreted the single rune, you can either decide it's not the best day for it and put your runes away, or if you're feeling good you can carry on with one of the other spreads in this chapter.

The single-rune draw is as simple as it sounds: shake your rune bag, draw one rune and place it in front of you. Read its interpretation then take some time to allow words, images and connections to form in your mind.

If you're drawing a daily rune you might like to try carrying the rune (for example, in your pocket or wallet) as a way of taking its guiding wisdom with you, or to help you ponder its meaning throughout the day. Also, notice if you draw the same rune multiple times in a week. That can be a tap on the shoulder that there's something in your life that needs closer attention.

Two-rune spread

This simple spread will help you weigh up the pros and cons of a situation. It's handy for getting a balanced view of a personal conflict, when contemplating a house move or job offer, or any other big decisions.

Set an intention to approach your dilemma with an open mind and a willingness to consider new perspectives. Simply draw two random runes and place them side by side. The rune on the left represents the Pros and the rune on the right is the Cons. Ponder what the runes symbolise for your situation and jot down your Pros and Cons list in your journal.

Three-rune spread

This classic rune reading looks at a scenario from past, present and future perspectives. It is an easy way to get an overview of a situation, such as a romantic relationship or your career journey. Draw three runes at random and lay them out in a row. Read them from left to right as you reflect on your intention.

1. **The past** – how your past actions and experiences have contributed to your question.
2. **The present** – the present situation and the challenges you may be facing.
3. **The future** – what's likely to happen if you continue your current course of action.

Six-rune spread

Known as the Runic Cross, this is a great one when you need a big dose of insight. It will give an in-depth overview of the situation, help uncover hopes and fears, identify any obstacles, then guide you towards figuring out how to move forward. It works best with simple, open-ended questions like, *How can I revamp my career? What do I need to know about my relationship? If I choose this path, what should I be aware of?*

Holding your question or intention in your mind, lay out the runes one by one in the formation below. Interpret the runes in the same order. Take your time, read the interpretations and let your intuition speak up.

1. The past and how it is influencing the present.
2. The present – what's going on right now.
3. Your future vision – your hopes and fears.
4. Your reasons for asking this question.
5. Obstacles and potential issues.
6. The eventual outcome.

The Square of Nine

Also known as The Magic Square, this reading takes the three-rune spread to a whole other level! It addresses past, present and future, but also helps to uncover the hidden stuff – the unconscious desires and motivations that could be influencing the situation at hand.

The square looks at eight different aspects then gives a prediction. The bottom row of runes addresses the past, the middle three focus on what's happening now, and the top row addresses the future. Use this spread when you're feeling stagnant or stuck. You'll figure out the obstacles getting in your way and how to move forward.

Choose nine runes at random then lay them out in order as per the diagram below. They should be read in this order too.

1. The past and its influence on the present.
2. Your general state of mind and attitude to the future.
3. Hidden motivations or desires may have influenced your life.
4. How these hidden influences will affect the outcome.
5. Your current circumstances.
6. Your stories, memories and beliefs about past events.
7. Your current attitude.
8. Hidden influences or past secrets.
9. The most desirable outcome.

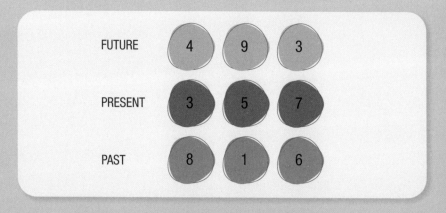

The meaning of runes

The following pages are a guide to all 25 runes. For each one you can discover its pronunciation, keywords, literal and symbolic meanings, plus insights on how to interpret them. Refer to this any time you need a helping hand to understand your readings but be sure to let your own impressions and ideas form first. Your intuition is a powerful and clever thing!

How do we know what the runes mean?
Much of the modern interpretation of runes is derived from ancient Norse wisdom, myths and legends, as well as a series of old rune poems. The three best-known poems are the Anglo-Saxon Rune Poem, the Old Norse Rune Poem, and the Icelandic Rune Poem.

While the interpretations in this book are influenced and inspired by this rich history, they are very much a modern take on the runes. Also, the more you work with runes the less you will need to turn to this guide, as your own impressions and interpretations will start to naturally emerge.

What happens if a rune is inverted?

When you randomly draw a rune from your rune bag and put it on the table, sometimes you may place it the wrong way up. This is known as an inverted or reversed rune and applies to 16 runes in the set. One example is Tiwaz, which is considered inverted when its arrow points downward instead of up.

Inverted runes have an alternative interpretation. Sometimes the meaning is the opposite of the upright and other times it's related. An inverted rune is not something to be alarmed about. Like an 'upside down' card in the tarot, it can indicate something in your life that needs attention, such as a challenge, an imbalance, or something you've been avoiding that you need to face. It's all very useful stuff to know!

Introducing the runes

The 24 runes of the Elder Futhark are divided into three categories of eight runes, known as an 'aett'.

1. **Frey's Aett** symbolises the basic ingredients of a happy, healthy and fulfilling life.
   Fehu, Uruz, Thurisaz, Ansuz, Raidho, Kenaz, Gebo, Wunjo
2. **Hagal's Aett** is all about life's challenging moments.
   Hagalaz, Naudhiz, Isa, Jera, Eihwaz, Perthro, Algiz, Sowilo
3. **Tyr's Aett** is associated with the experiences that shape being human.
   Tiwaz, Berkana, Ehwaz, Mannaz, Laguz, Ingwaz, Dagaz, Othala

Note: The blank rune known as Wyrd is a modern addition. While you can work with it alongside the other runes, it's not a part of the Elder Futhark. We'll explore this more later in the chapter (see page 94).

Runes at a glance

Rune	Name	Letter	Translation	Symbolic meanings
ᚠ	Fehu	F	Cattle, wealth	Prosperity, money, abundance, beginnings
ᚢ	Uruz	U	Ox, strength	Determination, strength, vitality, health
ᚦ	Thurisaz	Th	Thorn	Protection, warning, boundaries, disruption
ᚨ	Ansuz	A	God, mouth	Communication, word, divine inspiration, speech
ᚱ	Raidho	R	Wheel	Travel, time, movement, an inner journey
ᚲ	Kenaz	K	Torch	Fire, passion, warmth, energy, power, positivity
ᚷ	Gebo	G	Gift	Gifts, generosity, opportunity, commitment
ᚹ	Wunjo	W	Joy	Joy, pleasure, success, happy endings
ᚺ	Hagalaz	H	Hail	Disruption, forces outside our control, limitations, delays
ᚾ	Naudhiz	N	Need	Necessity, patience, hardship, a learning situation
ᛁ	Isa	I	Ice	Frozen, plans on hold, stillness, frustration
ᛃ	Jera	J	Harvest	Celebration, endings and beginnings, reaping rewards, life cycle
ᛇ	Eihwaz	E	Yew	Endings, progress, endurance, adaptability

Runes at a glance

Rune	Name	Letter	Translation	Symbolic meanings
ᚲ	Perthro	P	Cup	Mystery, randomness, coincidence, secrets uncovered
ᛉ	Algiz	Z	Elk	Protection, healing, support, self-interest, the wisdom of the universe
ᛊ	Sowilo	S	Sun	Energy, success, clarity, poetic justice
ᛏ	Tiwaz	T	Commitment	Sacrifice, victory, leadership, principles
ᛒ	Berkana	B	Birch	New beginnings, birth, fertility, family
ᛗ	Ehwaz	E	Horse	Partnership, trust, teamwork, motion
ᛘ	Mannaz	M	Human	Humanity, judgement, interdependence, collective potential
ᚱ	Laguz	L	Water, lake	Emotion, cleansing, flow, a safe haven
ᛝ	Ingwaz	Ng	Earth	Potential, new beginnings, fertility, growth
ᛞ	Dagaz	D	Dawn	Daylight, breakthrough, transformation, hope
ᛟ	Othala	O	Home	Heritage, responsibility, identity, loyalty
ᚹ	Wyrd	-	Fate	Fate, a blank slate, a leap into the unknown

Fehu

Pronunciation: Fey-hoo

Letter sound: F

Translation: Cattle, wealth

Themes: Prosperity, money, abundance, beginnings

Fehu is the rune of wealth. In ancient times owning cattle was a sign of success. Not only were cows tradable assets, but they also offered life-saving sustenance in times of need. So, while interpretations of Fehu usually focus on material possessions like money and property, the broader meaning is about abundance and prosperity across your whole life, from good health to professional and social success.

Depending on the context of your reading, Fehu can indicate that some good fortune is about to come your way. You may be about to reap the rewards of previous hard work in your business or career.

If you're already doing well in the financial department, Fehu is a handy reminder to receive your good fortune with grace and gratitude and to appreciate what you have rather than always wanting more. When Fehu pops up, remember that generosity is the key to avoiding greed. It feels good to share your abundance with others, whether that's donating to a worthy cause or buying a coffee for a stranger in the cafe queue.

Fehu can also symbolise new beginnings, like a new creative project, business venture or friendship.

Inverted meaning: Fehu reversed can indicate a financial or personal frustration or challenge. This can be the nudge you need to pause and regroup, to revisit your budget or shift your priorities.

FEHU

CATTLE
–
WEALTH

 Uruz

Pronunciation: Oo-rooze

Letter sound: U

Translation: Ox, strength

Themes: Determination, strength, vitality, health

Uruz is all about strength, power and primal energy. It's symbolised by the auroch, the wild ox that once roamed across Northern Europe. Unlike the domesticated cattle of Fehu, the auroch was fierce and untameable. It's a great reminder to, when appropriate, embrace your wild and determined side. It can be a powerful force of change and creativity.

Uruz is also about endurance and courage. If it appears in a reading when you're going through a tough time, be reassured that you have deep reserves of strength and power to weather the storm.

Uruz is also about health and vitality, both physical and metaphorical. If you've been struggling with illness, it can indicate that healing is on the way. If you're immersed in a project or going after a dream, Uruz hints that you're right on track and that you've got all the power, momentum and courage required to see it through to fruition. There's no stopping you!

Inverted meaning: Uruz in reverse can be a call for caution. An ox is a powerful and strong beast, but you don't want to be a bull in a china shop! Consider if there are situations where you need to use your words more wisely or to tame some wilder impulses.

Uruz inverted can also point to willpower or motivation, or a missed opportunity. What action could you take today to be a more dynamic and vivacious you?

Thurisaz

Pronunciation: Thoo-ree-saws

Letter sound: Th

Translation: Thorn

Themes: Protection, warning, boundaries, disruption

Symbolised by a thorn, the spiky nature of Thurisaz is a reminder of the importance of protection. You may be facing a challenging situation where you need to 'armour up' and have strong personal boundaries. Take the necessary precautions to make sure no one is taking advantage of you. Be mindful of areas where you're vulnerable or taking unnecessary risks.

The presence of Thurisaz can also be an alert that a challenging change or a disruption to the status quo is on the horizon. Rather than be alarmed, try to prepare for the unexpected and consider your options calmly and carefully. Remember that change can be a healthy thing!

This rune may show up in a reading if you're feeling defensive or under attack about a situation. While it's important to have your thorns at the ready for protection, try to recognise when they've become a block to connecting with your fellow humans.

Inverted meaning: Thurisaz in reverse may point to an unresolved issue, or a reluctance to deal with hardship. The thorn of Thurisaz is a blunt reminder that conflict and change are inevitable parts of life. While those spiky situations are painful to deal with, it's a much better option than letting them fester and become even more troublesome in the future.

THURISAZ

THORN

Ansuz

Pronunciation: Ahn-sooze

Letter sound: A

Translation: God, mouth

Themes: Communication, word, divine inspiration, speech

Ansuz is about the power of words and communication. Words are the tools we use to express our thoughts and share our needs, desires and struggles. When Ansuz appears in a reading it can be a reminder to speak with clarity and honesty; to calmly state your feelings to your loved ones and work colleagues, rather than expecting them to read your mind.

This rune is also associated with wisdom and divine communication. Pay attention to the sage advice offered up by those around you, as their experience can be hugely helpful. At the same time, Ansuz offers a nudge to listen out for the whispered words inside you, or to notice little coincidences that feel like signs from the universe. Sometimes that's where the biggest moments of insight and inspiration come from.

Ansuz can also be a call to action to use your voice. Is there an opinion that you're yearning to express or a story you want to tell? Whether it's a letter, a song, a poem, a social media post, or having an uncomfortable but much-needed conversation with a friend, tap into your inner wisdom to find the best words to say what you need to say.

Inverted meaning: Ansuz may point to a miscommunication, sending mixed messages or a reluctance to speak up. Consider if you need to use your words at all or to choose them more carefully when you do.

ANSUZ

GOD
—
MOUTH

Raidho

Pronunciation: Ray-doe

Letter sound: R

Translation: Wheel

Themes: Travel, time, movement, an inner journey

Raidho is a rune that's going places! It can signify a literal journey or an inner, metaphorical one. When Raidho appears in a reading, it can be a nice thumbs up from the universe that you're on the right path and an encouragement to keep going, even when the road gets bumpy. It's also a reminder to stay present and enjoy the journey, which might be just as rewarding as the destination.

Raidho represents new paths, new experiences and new ideas. In moments of doubt, you might feel like it would be easier to stay put, where everything is safe and familiar. But sometimes you need to be brave, stop worrying about what others think and just go for it!

Raidho also relates to the wheel, which reminds us that life is about cycles of change. This rune may pop up when you're in a transition from one stage of life to another, such as changing jobs or moving house. Remember that change is what keeps that wheel turning so you can keep growing and evolving.

Inverted meaning: You may be hesitating or waiting for the 'right time' or the 'right opportunity', rather than taking action on a choice or issue. There is no such thing as the perfect moment, so perhaps it's time to get the show on the road.

RAIDHO

WHEEL

Kenaz

Pronunciation: Kay-naz

Letter sound: K

Translation: Torch

Themes: Fire, passion, energy, enlightenment

Kenaz is a rune of enlightenment, especially of the spiritual kind. The clue is in the literal meaning 'torch'. When you find yourself stuck in the metaphorical cave, a torch will provide light in the darkness to help you see the situation with more clarity.

If you're in the midst of a puzzling or troubling situation, the appearance of Kenaz can mean you can expect a lightbulb moment soon or that you will soon see the light at the end of the tunnel.

Kenaz is also about manifestation and energy – your inner fire. You can light a powerful spark with your thoughts and energy will flow in the direction of your efforts and attention. Kenaz is a reminder that you have all you need to bring that dream project to life, to pursue an opportunity or to take on a new challenge.

While fire can provide warmth and illumination, remember that it can also be a destructive force. Kenaz may point to something in your life that needs to end or be destroyed before new growth can happen.

Inverted meaning: It may be that a flame has gone out and that something in your life is coming to an end. The key is to decide if there're still some faint embers that are worth taking the time to rekindle or if it is time to gracefully let go and embrace the lessons the situation has taught you.

KENAZ

TORCH

Gebo

Pronunciation: Gey-bo

Letter sound: G

Translation: Gift

Themes: Gifts, generosity, opportunity, commitment

Gebo is all about gifts, generosity and relationships. Whether it's a partner, family member, friend or colleague, Gebo shines a light on your connections. It's a reminder that a healthy relationship is a reciprocal one. This rune is an invitation to examine your connections and ask if they have a balanced exchange of energy.

Depending on the context of the reading, you may need to look out for situations where you are giving more than you receive. Feeling depleted or resentful is always a clue that the relationship may not be on equal footing.

Alternatively, Gebo may be asking you to look at your own role in the dynamics of a relationship. Make sure you're not hogging the stage while offering little in return.

Sometimes Gebo in a reading can be more literal. A lucky break may be on the horizon or you might receive a surprise gift. This may be a physical gift or something intangible, such as an offer of emotional support.

Gebo is also about your innate gifts. You may unearth a new natural talent or take a favourite pastime to a new level. Drawing this rune is a sign to make sure you're embracing your skills and putting them to good use.

X

GEBO

GIFT

Wunjo

Pronunciation: Woon-you

Letter sound: W

Translation: Joy

Themes: Joy, pleasure, success, happy endings

Wunjo is the rune of joy. Do a happy dance if you draw this one! It may signal the arrival of good news, a period of balance and bliss, a happy ending to a difficult situation or an exciting beginning. This may be your reward for past hard work and sacrifices, so be sure to savour the moment!

If Wunjo has appeared in the context of a reading about love, it tends to mean that you're about to enjoy some particularly happy moments. An existing relationship will feel strengthened or if you're single you might soon make an intriguing new connection.

If you've found yourself caught up in a cycle of negative thinking, Wunjo can be a reminder that happiness is something you can generate from within. Start by practising gratitude and actively seeking moments of joy. Can you make time for a few things that put a smile on your dial? What obligations could you ditch from your to-do list? Give it a go and you'll soon notice your thought patterns shifting in a more positive and optimistic direction.

Inverted meaning: You may be experiencing a mental block, a feeling of stagnation or be caught up in a conflict. This is the time to go kindly and put any important decisions or conversations on hold until you are in better spirits.

Hagalaz

Pronunciation: Horg-a-laws

Letter sound: H

Translation: Hail

Themes: Disruption, forces outside our control, limitations, delays

There's no avoiding it: Hagalaz represents hail. If you've ever been caught in a hailstorm you'll know all too well, it can do a little damage!

But remember that no hailstorm lasts forever. Hailstones eventually turn back into water, the substance that nourishes all living things. So, while Hagalaz does point to the possibility of challenging events, delays or obstacles, it also indicates that things will bounce back eventually. A hailstorm may decimate your rose bushes, but it can also give your lawn a much-needed drink.

When Hagalaz appears in a reading, it can be about the unpredictability of nature. There may be a crisis taking place in your life. Despite your efforts to stay in control, this may be an occasion when you need to let go of the reins. When forces are beyond your command, all you can do is let things happen, be patient and calm, and know you have the inner resources and perseverance to recover and rebuild.

Hagalaz can be a reminder that if events don't unfold in the way you wanted them to, there can be gifts in the way they did. You may learn valuable lessons, see things from a refreshed perspective or find an exciting new direction to explore.

HAGALAZ

HAIL

Naudhiz

Pronunciation: Naw-theez

Letter sound: N

Translation: Need

Themes: Necessity, patience, hardship, a learning situation

Naudhiz is all about need and necessity. When the rune shows up in a reading, it can indicate that something in your life is not fulfilling you or meeting your needs. This could be a sudden demand, an ongoing hardship, a material lack or an emotional dissatisfaction. These situations may leave you feeling frustrated, constrained or struggling to move forward.

Symbolically, Naudhiz resembles two sticks rubbing together to create fire. This is a great reminder that, with effort, you can create a spark. In this way, this rune can be a sobering wake-up call that big action is required in the midst of a testing time. There is no other option if you want things to change.

Naudhiz urges you to dig deep as you meet your challenges and not let despair overwhelm you. Know that the difficult times can be the ones that we look back on and realise, That's where the huge growth took place. That's where my true character was forged. Those obstacles I faced turned out to be opportunities to stretch in a new direction.

Of course, these kinds of statements can be somewhat irritating to hear when you're right in the thick of a struggle! But know that the appearance of Naudhiz is a whisper that you will get through these hard times and emerge stronger than ever.

Isa

Pronunciation: EE-sah

Letter sound: I

Translation: Ice

Themes: Frozen, plans on hold, stillness, frustration

Associated with ice, Isa is an indication that something is blocked or frozen. A project may have ground to a halt, negotiations may have stalled, or you may be emotionally or energetically stuck.

Isa is asking you not to fight it. This is a time to be still and patient. Save your energy because forward movement is just not possible right now. Make like a glacier and take things slowly.

While Isa can point to frustration and discomfort, this period of stillness may end up being a blessing in disguise. Stepping back may change your perspective, cooling off a previously heated situation.

If your reading is about a relationship, Isa can point to one that's entered a frosty period, with distant communication or cooled affections. Again, this is not time for hasty words or actions. Take some time to reflect on this connection and decide if you're willing to put in the energy it would take to defrost relations or if you want to let this one float by.

Don't forget that ice can also act as a preservative. Isa may be showing you that there is something in your life that needs your attention, a bit of rest and repair, in order to ensure its longevity.

I

ISA

ICE

Jera

Pronunciation: YAY-rah

Letter sound: J

Translation: Harvest

Themes: Celebration, endings and beginnings, reaping rewards, life cycle

Jera is the rune of celebrating a good harvest. It is the embodiment of the phrase, 'you reap what you sow'.

When Jera appears, it can mean you're about to enjoy the bounty of the seeds you planted long ago. All that nurturing, determination and patience has finally paid off. This could be in the form of good news, a creative project finally coming to life, an important contract signed or a big project successfully completed. It's time to celebrate a job well done and acknowledge how far you have come.

If you're going through adversity, Jera can signal that you're moving into a period of hope and light. You may soon be able to put difficult times or unpleasant memories behind you.

Seasonality is another theme of Jera. In nature, the growing seasons are followed by the colder months of rest and hibernation. This can be a reminder to strive for that same balance.

Jera is also the origin of the modern word 'year' and speaks to the endlessly cyclical nature of life. While it's important to celebrate those good harvests when they happen, you can't afford to rest on your laurels for long. Time rolls on and so must you. Think about the lessons you have learnt from this season and how you can build on them in the next one. That's how you keep growing and evolving.

JERA

HARVEST

Eihwaz

Pronunciation: Ee-warz

Letter sound: E

Translation: Yew

Themes: Endings, progress, endurance, adaptability

Eihwaz is associated with endings, which are a natural, inevitable and important part of life. This rune may pop up in your reading as a chapter of your life is ending.

Things may have been quiet or even a little stagnant for a long while, but suddenly, change is in the air. Perhaps you're ready to shed old parts of yourself, to leave a bad habit or two behind, to tie up some loose ends or to move on from a relationship.

Don't hold on to what no longer serves you. Trust that deep down intuition that it's time to let go. As painful as it can be, the good news is that endings create space for new beginnings. While Eihwaz has associations with death, this is at heart an optimistic rune that's all about possibilities, progress and rebirth. You are heading into an exciting new phase, so gather your courage, be patient and let it unfold.

Eihwaz also represents the yew, a symbol of endurance. This clever tree is known for its incredible longevity and capacity to regenerate from its own trunk. Its wood is super strong yet remarkably flexible. Like this iconic tree, you can be strong while knowing when to bend and go with the flow. Eihwaz is confident that you can take on this new chapter and thrive.

EIHWAZ

YEW

Perthro

Pronunciation: Pear-throw

Letter sound: P

Translation: Cup

Themes: Mystery, randomness, coincidence, secrets uncovered

The most enigmatic of all the runes, Perthro is about hidden knowledge. It speaks to mystery, secrets and spooky coincidences. A situation that has been puzzling or unknown may soon be explained. There could be a revelation of some kind, someone may spill a secret that they have been keeping or a surprising new piece of information will provide the answer to a frustrating conundrum.

Most likely the knowledge uncovered will come in the form of a juicy insight from your intuition. Be on the lookout for subtle signals and signs. Try switching off your phone for a while, practising some meditation or simply going for a quiet walk. This will give you the space you need to tune into that wise voice inside that instinctively knows what's best for you.

This is a particularly good time to work with runes more regularly, or other forms of divination, as you'll be particularly open to their wisdom.

Inverted meaning: Perthro in the inverted position can be a warning that you're being pulled off course, letting trivial matters distract you from what's really important. While it's good to take the opinions and experiences of others into consideration, you know yourself best. Perthro is a reminder that you really can trust your inner wisdom.

Algiz

Pronunciation: All-geez

Letter sound: Z

Translation: Elk

Themes: Protection, healing, support, self-interest, the wisdom of the Universe

Algiz is the rune of protection. It is symbolised by the elk, which uses its powerful antlers for warding off its foes. The appearance of Algiz can be a nudge to check in with your own protection levels. Make sure you are taking care of your physical and emotional needs and not overextending yourself, which could leave you vulnerable.

Algiz can indicate that you are indeed protected right now, making it a safe time to explore some new horizons. Sign up for that class you've dreamed about, visit somewhere new or take up an exciting new hobby.

Willpower is another characteristic of Algiz. If you've been wanting to dedicate yourself to study, train for your first marathon or kick an unhealthy habit like smoking, this is a thumbs-up from the universe that you will find the gumption to stick it out.

Inverted meaning: Algiz inverted doubles down on the message of taking care of yourself right now. Remember that old saying about putting on your own oxygen mask first – that's not a selfish thing to do. It may be that other people are making a lot of demands on you and not even noticing that you're on the edge of burnout. Algiz is the permission to go into self-preservation mode. Slow down, put your feet up and replenish those energy stores.

ALGIZ

ELK

Sowilo

Pronunciation: So-wee-lo

Letter sound: S

Translation: Sun

Themes: Energy, success, clarity, poetic justice

Sowilo is the rune of the sun, celebrating its light and life-giving magic. It represents the light of day, when all the dark corners get illuminated and the path ahead becomes clear.

If you're in the midst of a tough time, Sowilo is a reminder that even after the darkest days the light will return. If you've been wrestling with a big decision, it shines a light on the situation and guides you towards the best option.

Sowilo is a happy and hopeful rune to encounter. Some even say it's the best rune to encounter! It can indicate a successful outcome, such as a triumphant work project, a boost of warmth and energy in a relationship, or a fair and just outcome to a legal matter.

With the sun's healing rays, health is another big theme for Sowilo. It often indicates a happy resolution to a physical issue or a strong recovery after illness.

Alongside all this lovely positivity, we can't forget that there is such a thing as too much sun. Depending on the context of your reading, it may be a nudge to look at how and where you're directing your energy. You may be overdoing it or pushing your luck a little in an area of your life. It could be time to cool off for a while to make sure you don't fly too close to that big fireball in the sky.

 # Tiwaz

Pronunciation: Tee-warz

Letter sound: T

Translation: Commitment

Themes: Sacrifice, victory, leadership, principles

Symbolised by an upwardly pointing arrow, Tiwaz is about justice, leadership and doing what is right.

When this rune appears, it can hint at making a sacrifice for the greater good. You may be called upon to put your personal ambitions aside for the moment to do something that's more urgent or important right now. You may need to take care of a loved one who is ill or make a compromise in a relationship or at work.

While it may feel frustrating, the rewards will be rich in the long run and you will earn the respect and gratitude of others for your efforts.

Tiwaz is also about integrity, fairness and staying true to your convictions. When taking action, it's important that you stick to your principles and don't stray from your values.

Tiwaz is also encouraging you to go after your goals right now with courage and commitment. The theme of sacrifice pops up again: you may need to make a time or financial sacrifice, but it will be worth it to make your dreams happen.

Inverted meaning: The downward pointing arrow can indicate a loss of confidence, hope or direction. The advice from Tiwaz is the same as the upright meaning: stay true to your convictions and take steady action, because you have all the power within you to make it happen.

Berkana

Pronunciation: Bair-kah-nah

Letter sound: B

Translation: Birch

Themes: New beginnings, birth, fertility, family

Berkana is the rune of new beginnings and birth. Its appearance can be a great omen for a new life chapter, like a budding relationship, a career change, starting a business, moving home or a big family event. It can also be literal, representing the birth of a child.

Berkana is translated as the birch tree, a symbol of fertility and regeneration. It can be a lovely sign of hope that a missed opportunity may come round again, or that a strained relationship will be rekindled.

Infused with maternal energy, Berkana is also a reminder to nurture all this newness so it can grow into something healthy and strong. Take tender care of yourself too – don't skimp on self-care and reach out for emotional support if you need it. Berkana suggests that your loved ones will be there for you.

Berkana is also about female energy and healing, celebrating the body's incredible powers of renewal. If you have been ill, you may be on the road to recovery and feeling like yourself again.

Inverted meaning: There may be family conflicts with harsh words or frazzled tempers. Someone may be resistant to your offers of help. Try not to catastrophise and make sure you're not expecting someone to behave in a way that you'd prefer, as opposed to accepting them for who they are.

BERKANA

BIRCH

 Ehwaz

Pronunciation: Eh-waz

Letter sound: E

Translation: Horse

Themes: Partnership, trust, teamwork, motion

Ehwaz is represented by a horse, which was a sacred animal to the Vikings. A successful partnership between horse and rider is all about faith, trust and teamwork, and this rune reminds us that we need those same qualities to make our own relationships work.

If Ehwaz pops up, there may be a situation where the team needs to come together, like a big work project or a family event. With mutual respect, cooperation and hard work you can pull in the same direction, get the momentum going and achieve amazing things.

Ehwaz can also be shining a light on your relationship with yourself. If your confidence is having a wobbly moment and you're doubting your abilities, this is a time to be kind. When you catch yourself having unhelpful thoughts, gently challenge them and remember the unique skills and qualities you possess.

Travel and movement are also big themes of Ehwaz. It could be a physical journey but more likely an inner transformation is taking place. Notice the ways you're changing and enjoy the ride!

Inverted meaning: If you're sensing that someone is not entirely trustworthy, Eihwaz can be a nod that your instincts are spot on. On the other hand, it may simply be that your defences are up. Check in that you're not letting past painful events dictate the situation.

M

EHWAZ

HORSE

Mannaz

Pronunciation: Mah-nawz

Letter sound: M

Translation: Human

Themes: Humanity, judgement, interdependence, collective potential

Mannaz represents both humankind and the individual self. It celebrates all that is unique about us humans – like our creativity, innovation, intelligence and adaptability – as well as our shared experiences and values. Mannaz reminds us that we are interdependent beings. We need each other to reach our full potential and we're more powerful when we help each other.

At the same time, Mannaz represents the individual. We can't always depend on others after all, and self-reliance and independence are excellent qualities too.

Mannaz can be a nudge to look at the balance between your individual needs and those of your community. Perhaps you've taken on too much and need to schedule some rest or to ask for help. Or perhaps you've been wrapped in your own world and are only just noticing a loved one quietly struggling. Reach out to them with some kind words, a listening ear and/or some home baking. Even better, take care of some errands on their to-do list. We're all imperfect beings and we have to look out for each other!

Inverted meaning: You may be feeling isolated, like you're not fitting in with your social group or that you're not meeting expectations with someone. Gently check in with the facts to see if this is actually true or if you might be projecting an inner conflict. Take some time to meditate or journal to figure it out.

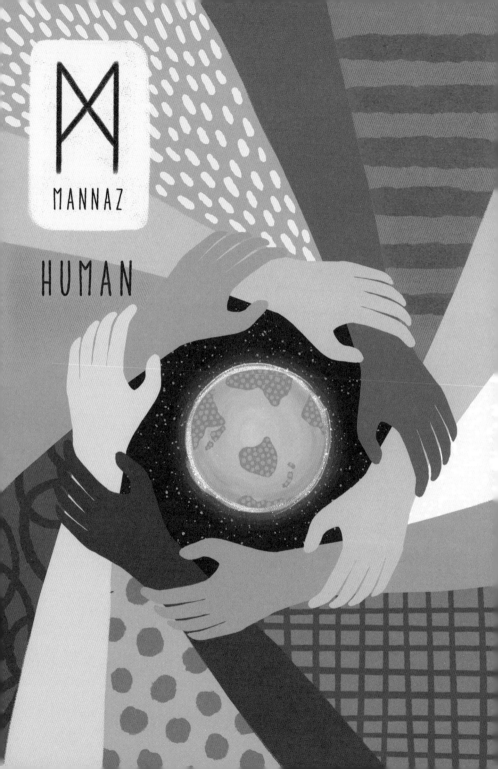

Laguz

Pronunciation: La-gooze

Letter sound: L

Translation: Water, lake

Themes: Emotion, cleansing, flow, a safe haven

Laguz symbolises water and emotions. The ebb and flow of water echo the ever-changing tide of our emotional state.

When Laguz is drawn, you may have unexpressed feelings beneath the surface that you've tried to keep a lid on. This rune is a permission slip to let those tears fall. These waves of emotion can be your intuition trying to tell you something that could help you solve a problem or to make a big decision.

If you're in a stressful situation, Laguz is an encouragement to be flexible and 'go with the flow'. It can even mean a literal call to seek out water for its healing magic. Whether it's heading to the pool for a swim or meditating by the sea, water can bring clarity and peace.

Laguz also speaks to taking a step out of your comfort zone with a new job or an adventurous trip. Just as the Vikings set sail into unknown seas, this may be the time for you to take a chance and seek a new horizon.

Inverted meaning: You may be feeling consumed by stormy emotions, like impatience, anger or resentment. Try to take a deep breath and step away from the situation to get some perspective.

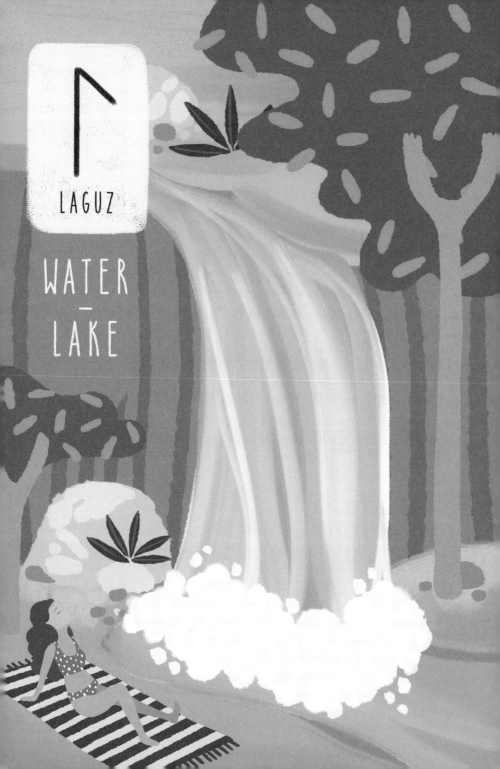

LAGUZ

WATER
–
LAKE

Ingwaz

Pronunciation: Ing-warz

Letter sound: Ng

Translation: Earth

Themes: Potential, new beginnings, fertility, growth

Ingwaz symbolises fertility and sexuality. The appearance of Ingwaz can signal the start of a phase of life where it feels like lush and exciting things are suddenly happening.

There might be a challenging new job opportunity, a thrilling and passionate relationship, or a period of creativity and productivity where great ideas seem to crackle in the air around you.

Ingwaz is also about new beginnings and stepping into your full potential. Right now, you may be shedding an old skin and a new and improved version of you is emerging. This can feel exhilarating but a bit scary at the same time. You may worry that you won't be able to handle a new opportunity or that you'll regret making a big move. But this is a time for bold and courageous action, even if the new beginning is in an unknown area.

Ingwaz is a sign to let go of old patterns, behaviours, people or things to make room for new experiences. What you'll gain in the future will more than make up for what you're leaving behind.

Don't let fear of success hold you back either. Ingwaz deeply believes that it's time to let your light shine.

INGWAZ

EARTH

Dagaz

Pronunciation: Dah-gaz

Letter sound: D

Translation: Dawn

Themes: Daylight, breakthrough, transformation, hope

Dagaz represents the dawn and the power of a new day. Daybreak, the moment when the darkness of night transforms into day, brings new hope and a chance to start again. This makes Dagaz a positive and hopeful rune to encounter. If you're going through a period of sadness or frustration, it is signalling that better times are ahead.

This rune is also associated with a breakthrough, where you bust through whatever barriers or self-imposed limitations that have held you back. There could be a delicious jolt of creative inspiration, an 'ah-ha' moment that sparks a new direction, a sudden solution to a puzzling problem or a peaceful resolution to a tense situation.

Dagaz is also about transitions. If you have been thinking of a career switch, this is a great time to learn a new skill or begin some study to get you started on that new path. If you've been struggling with a troubling issue like an addiction, a phobia or debt, it's an ideal time to face it and reach out for help.

Dagaz promises that the sun is shining on you and that change is possible if you have faith. But you will need to put in the work as it won't be a one-time effort. Just like the dawn, rise up again each day and keep going!

DAGAZ

DAWN

Othala

Pronunciation: Oh-tha-lah

Letter sound: O

Translation: Home

Themes: Heritage, responsibility, identity, loyalty

Othala symbolises home, family, belonging and the legacy we receive from our ancestors. This may be a reminder to appreciate or accept what your family has passed down to you through the generations. It concerns both material and inherent attributes, from wisdom, culture, traditions, beliefs, to facial features, personality quirks, talents and mannerisms.

Othala can represent a struggle with identity. You may feel like your family is stifling you, or there's a clash of values, and you need some distance to be able to spread your wings.

In contrast, Othala can also signal a homecoming. After a period of rebellion or escape, you may have a new appreciation for what is good about where you came from and be ready to return to home base as your adult self.

Othala can indicate a happy time for home and family life. There may be improvements in financial or emotional matters or good health news for an older family member. When Othala appears, it can also be an excellent time for buying or selling a home, spending time with loved ones, or kicking off a home renovation.

Inverted meaning: There may be family issues to deal with, such as estrangement, financial disagreements or resentment about someone not pulling their weight to help in a difficult situation. Take a time out when needed and think carefully before you speak because no one holds a grudge quite like your own kin.

Wyrd

Pronunciation: Werd

Letter sound: Not applicable

Translation: Fate

Themes: Fate, a blank slate, a leap into the unknown

Known as the rune of fate, Wyrd is a modern addition to the 24 runes of the Elder Futhark and is completely blank.

Your rune set may or may not include Wyrd, and it's entirely a personal choice as to whether you use it. There is no historical evidence that blank runes were ever used, but many people find it to be a very useful addition to their practice.

If you draw Wyrd as a single rune it's said to mean it's not a good day for working with runes, so put it back in your bag and try another reading tomorrow.

If Wyrd shows up in a multi-rune spread it points to fate – that the outcome as you interpret it is meant to be. Depending on the context of the reading and the surrounding runes, it could also indicate a leap into the unknown or that there is something you're not yet meant to know.

The blankness of Wyrd can also be a message to look to your inner wisdom. It may simply mean you need to take more time to contemplate your options.

Another interpretation is that the blankness of Wyrd is a reminder that life is essentially a blank slate and you have the power to write your future on it. In this way, Wyrd can be a rather optimistic and hopeful rune, so why not add it to your rune bag and see if it has anything to say?

WYRD

FATE

Conclusion

Runes are a simple yet deeply satisfying form of modern divination. The mysterious lines and shapes of this ancient practice still speak to the joys and struggles of our lives today.

Now that you know how runes can help, remember to practise regularly and be patient. It doesn't matter if you're a casual dabbler or a deep-dive devotee, just approach them with an open mind and heart. Let the runes share their wisdom and shine a light on your own.

Whether you seek a quick dose of insight to start your day or a detailed analysis of your life, think of the runes as wise and trusty friends that you can check in with at any time. Timeless insights and 'ah-ha' moments are always just a shake of the rune bag away.

Enjoy your journey!